The Poetry of Algernon Charles Swinburne

VOLUME XVI - THE TALE OF BALEN

Algernon Charles Swinburne was born on April 5th, 1837, in London, into a wealthy Northumbrian family. He was educated at Eton and at Balliol College, Oxford, but did not complete a degree.

In 1860 Swinburne published two verse dramas but achieved his first literary success in 1865 with Atalanta in Calydon, written in the form of classical Greek tragedy. The following year "Poems and Ballads" brought him instant notoriety. He was now identified with "indecent" themes and the precept of art for art's sake.

Although he produced much after this success in general his popularity and critical reputation declined. The most important qualities of Swinburne's work are an intense lyricism, his intricately extended and evocative imagery, metrical virtuosity, rich use of assonance and alliteration, and bold, complex rhythms.

Swinburne's physical appearance was small, frail, and plagued by several other oddities of physique and temperament. Throughout the 1860s and 1870s he drank excessively and was prone to accidents that often left him bruised, bloody, or unconscious. Until his forties he suffered intermittent physical collapses that necessitated removal to his parents' home while he recovered.

Throughout his career Swinburne also published literary criticism of great worth. His deep knowledge of world literatures contributed to a critical style rich in quotation, allusion, and comparison. He is particularly noted for discerning studies of Elizabethan dramatists and of many English and French poets and novelists. As well he was a noted essayist and wrote two novels.

In 1879, Swinburne's friend and literary agent, Theodore Watts-Dunton, intervened during a time when Swinburne was dangerously ill. Watts-Dunton isolated Swinburne at a suburban home in Putney and gradually weaned him from alcohol, former companions and many other habits as well.

Much of his poetry in this period may be inferior but some individual poems are exceptional; "By the North Sea," "Evening on the Broads," "A Nympholept," "The Lake of Gaube," and "Neap-Tide."

Swinburne lived another thirty years with Watts-Dunton. He denied Swinburne's friends access to him, controlled the poet's money, and restricted his activities. It is often quoted that 'he saved the man but killed the poet'.

Swinburne died on April 10th, 1909 at the age of seventy-two.

Index of Contents

Algernon Charles Swinburne – A Concise Bibliography

TO MY MOTHER

Love that holds life and death in fee,
Deep as the clear unsounded sea
And sweet as life or death can be,
Lays here my hope, my heart, and me
Before you, silent, in a song.
Since the old wild tale, made new, found grace,
When half sung through, before your face,
It needs must live a springtide space,
While April suns grow strong.

March 24, 1896.

THE TALE OF BALEN

I

In hawthorn-time the heart grows light,
The world is sweet in sound and sight,
Glad thoughts and birds take flower and flight,
The heather kindles toward the light,
    The whin is frankincense and flame.
And be it for strife or be it for love
The falcon quickens as the dove
When earth is touched from heaven above
    With joy that knows no name.

And glad in spirit and sad in soul
With dream and doubt of days that roll
As waves that race and find no goal
Rode on by bush and brake and bole
    A northern child of earth and sea.
The pride of life before him lay
Radiant: the heavens of night and day
Shone less than shone before his way
    His ways and days to be.

And all his life of blood and breath
Sang out within him: time and death

Were even as words a dreamer saith
When sleep within him slackeneth,
   And light and life and spring were one.
The steed between his knees that sprang,
The moors and woods that shone and sang,
The hours where through the spring's breath rang,
   Seemed ageless as the sun.

But alway through the bounteous bloom
That earth gives thanks if heaven illume
His soul forefelt a shadow of doom,
His heart foreknew a gloomier gloom
   Than closes all men's equal ways,
Albeit the spirit of life's light spring
With pride of heart upheld him, king
And lord of hours like snakes that sting
   And nights that darken days.

And as the strong spring round him grew
Stronger, and all blithe winds that blew
Blither, and flowers that flowered anew
More glad of sun and air and dew,
   The shadow lightened on his soul
And brightened into death and died
Like winter, as the bloom waxed wide
From woodside on to riverside
   And southward goal to goal.

Along the wandering ways of Tyne,
By beech and birch and thorn that shine
And laugh when life's requickening wine
Makes night and noon and dawn divine
   And stirs in all the veins of spring,
And past the brightening banks of Tees,
He rode as one that breathes and sees
A sun more blithe, a merrier breeze,
   A life that hails him king.

And down the softening south that knows
No more how glad the heather glows,
Nor how, when winter's clarion blows
Across the bright Northumbrian snows,
   Sea-mists from east and westward meet,
Past Avon senseless yet of song
And Thames that bore but swans in throng
He rode elate in heart and strong
   In trust of days as sweet.

So came he through to Camelot,
Glad, though for shame his heart waxed hot,
For hope within it withered not
To see the shaft it dreamed of shot
  Fair toward the glimmering goal of fame,
And all King Arthur's knightliest there
Approved him knightly, swift to dare
And keen to bid their records bear
  Sir Balen's northern name.

Sir Balen of Northumberland
Gat grace before the king to stand
High as his heart was, and his hand
Wrought honour toward the strange north strand
  That sent him south so goodly a knight.
And envy, sick with sense of sin,
Began as poisonous herbs begin
To work in base men's blood, akin
  To men's of nobler might.

And even so fell it that his doom,
For all his bright life's kindling bloom
And light that took no thought for gloom,
Fell as a breath from the opening tomb
  Full on him ere he wist or thought.
For once a churl of royal seed,
King Arthur's kinsman, faint in deed
And loud in word that knew not heed,
  Spake shame where shame was nought.

"What doth one here in Camelot
Whose birth was northward? Wot we not
As all his brethren borderers wot
How blind of heart, how keen and hot,
  The wild north lives and hates the south?
Men of the narrowing march that knows
Nought save the strength of storms and snows,
What would these carles where knighthood blows
  A trump of kinglike mouth?"

Swift from his place leapt Balen, smote
The liar across his face, and wrote
His wrath in blood upon the bloat
Brute cheek that challenged shame for note
  How vile a king-born knave might be.
Forth sprang their swords, and Balen slew
The knave ere well one witness knew
Of all that round them stood or drew

What sight was there to see.

Then spake the great king's wrathful will
A doom for six dark months to fill
Wherein close prison held him, still
And steadfast-souled for good or ill.
    But when those weary days lay dead
His lordliest knights and barons spake
Before the king for Balen's sake
Good speech and wise, of force to break
    The bonds that bowed his head.

II

In linden-time the heart is high
For pride of summer passing by
With lordly laughter in her eye;
A heavy splendour in the sky
    Uplifts and bows it down again.
The spring had waned from wood and wold
Since Balen left his prison hold
And lowlier-hearted than of old
    Beheld it wax and wane.

Though humble heart and poor array
Kept not from spirit and sense away
Their noble nature, nor could slay
The pride they bade but pause and stay
    Till time should bring its trust to flower,
Yet even for noble shame's sake, born
Of hope that smiled on hate and scorn,
He held him still as earth ere morn
    Ring forth her rapturous hour.

But even as earth when dawn takes flight
And beats her wings of dewy light
Full in the faltering face of night,
His soul awoke to claim by right
    The life and death of deed and doom,
When once before the king there came
A maiden clad with grief and shame
And anguish burning her like flame
    That feeds on flowers in bloom.

Beneath a royal mantle, fair
With goodly work of lustrous vair,
Girt fast against her side she bare

A sword whose weight bade all men there
   Quail to behold her face again.
Save of a passing perfect knight
Not great alone in force and fight
It might not be for any might
   Drawn forth, and end her pain.

So said she: then King Arthur spake:
"Albeit indeed I dare not take
Such praise on me, for knighthood's sake
And love of ladies will I make
   Assay if better none may be."
By girdle and by sheath he caught
The sheathed and girded sword, and wrought
With strength whose force availed him nought
   To save and set her free.

Again she spake: "No need to set
The might that man has matched not yet
Against it: he whose hand shall get
Grace to release the bonds that fret
   My bosom and my girdlestead
With little strain of strength or strife
Shall bring me as from death to life
And win to sister or to wife
   Fame that outlives men dead."

Then bade the king his knights assay
This mystery that before him lay
And mocked his might of manhood. "Nay,"
Quoth she, "the man that takes away
   This burden laid on me must be
A knight of record clean and fair
As sunlight and the flowerful air,
By sire and mother born to bear
   A name to shame not me."

Then forth strode Launcelot, and laid
The mighty-moulded hand that made
Strong knights reel back like birds affrayed
By storm that smote them as they strayed
   Against the hilt that yielded not.
Then Tristram, bright and sad and kind
As one that bore in noble mind
Love that made light as darkness blind,
   Fared even as Launcelot.

Then Lamoracke, with hardier cheer,

As one that held all hope and fear
Wherethrough the spirit of man may steer
In life and death less dark or dear,
 Laid hand thereon, and fared as they.
With half a smile his hand he drew
Back from the spell-bound thing, and threw
With half a glance his heart anew
 Toward no such blameless may.

Between Iseult and Guenevere
Sat one of name as high to hear,
But darklier doomed than they whose cheer
Foreshowed not yet the deadlier year
 That bids the queenliest head bow down,
The queen Morgause of Orkney: they
With scarce a flash of the eye could say
The very word of dawn, when day
 Gives earth and heaven their crown.

But bright and dark as night or noon
And lowering as a storm-flushed moon
When clouds and thwarting winds distune
The music of the midnight, soon
 To die from darkening star to star
And leave a silence in the skies
That yearns till dawn find voice and rise,
Shone strange as fate Morgause, with eyes
 That dwelt on days afar.

A glance that shot on Lamoracke
As from a storm-cloud bright and black.
Fire swift and blind as death's own track
Turned fleet as flame on Arthur back
 From him whose hand forsook the hilt:
And one in blood and one in sin
Their hearts caught fire of pain within
And knew no goal for them to win
 But death that guerdons guilt.

Then Gawain, sweet of soul and gay
As April ere he dreams of May,
Strove, and prevailed not: then Sir Kay,
The snake-souled envier, vile as they
 That fawn and foam and lurk and lie,
Sire of the bastard band whose brood
Was alway found at servile feud
With honour, faint and false and lewd,
 Scarce grasped and put it by.

Then wept for woe the damsel bound
With iron and with anguish round,
That none to help her grief was found
Or loose the inextricably inwound
   Grim curse that girt her life with grief
And made a burden of her breath,
Harsh as the bitterness of death.
Then spake the king as one that saith
   Words bitterer even than brief.

"Methought the wide round world could bring
Before the face of queen or king
No knights more fit for fame to sing
Than fill this full Round Table's ring
   With honour higher than pride of place:
But now my heart is wrung to know,
Damsel, that none whom fame can show
Finds grace to heal or help thy woe:
   God gives them not the grace."

Then from the lowliest place thereby,
With heart-enkindled cheek and eye
Most like the star and kindling sky
That say the sundawn's hour is high
   When rapture trembles through the sea,
Strode Balen in his poor array
Forth, and took heart of grace to pray
The damsel suffer even him to assay
   His power to set her free.

Nay, how should he avail, she said,
Averse with scorn-averted head,
Where these availed not? none had sped
Of all these mightier men that led
   The lists wherein he might not ride,
And how should less men speed? But he,
With lordlier pride of courtesy,
Put forth his hand and set her free
   From pain and humbled pride.

But on the sword he gazed elate
With hope set higher than fear or fate,
Or doubt of darkling days in wait;
And when her thankful praise waxed great
   And craved of him the sword again,
He would not give it. "Nay, for mine
It is till force may make it thine."

A smile that shone as death may shine
  Spake toward him bale and bane.

Strange lightning flickered from her eyes.
"Gentle and good in knightliest guise
And meet for quest of strange emprise
Thou hast here approved thee: yet not wise
  To keep the sword from me, I wis.
For with it thou shalt surely slay
Of all that look upon the day
The man best loved of thee, and lay
  Thine own life down for his."

"What chance God sends, that chance I take,"
He said. Then soft and still she spake;
"I would but for thine only sake
Have back the sword of thee, and break
  The links of doom that bind thee round.
But seeing thou wilt not have it so,
My heart for thine is wrung with woe."
"God's will," quoth he, "it is, we know,
  Wherewith our lives are bound."

"Repent it must thou soon," she said,
"Who wouldst not hear the rede I read
For thine and not for my sake, sped
In vain as waters heavenward shed
  From springs that falter and depart
Earthward. God bids not thee believe
Truth, and the web thy life must weave
For even this sword to close and cleave
  Hangs heavy round my heart."

So passed she mourning forth. But he,
With heart of springing hope set free
As birds that breast and brave the sea,
Bade horse and arms and armour be
  Made straightway ready toward the fray.
Nor even might Arthur's royal prayer
Withhold him, but with frank and fair
Thanksgiving and leave-taking there
  He turned him thence away.

III

As the east wind, when the morning's breast
Gleams like a bird's that leaves the nest,

A fledgeling halcyon's bound on quest,
Drives wave on wave on wave to west
 Till all the sea be life and light,
So time's mute breath, that brings to bloom
All flowers that strew the dead spring's tomb,
Drives day on day on day to doom
 Till all man's day be night.

Brief as the breaking of a wave
That hurls on man his thunderous grave
Ere fear find breath to cry or crave
Life that no chance may spare or save,
 The light of joy and glory shone
Even as in dreams where death seems dead
Round Balen's hope-exalted head,
Shone, passed, and lightened as it fled
 The shadow of doom thereon.

For as he bound him thence to fare,
Before the stately presence there
A lady like a windflower fair,
Girt on with raiment strange and rare
 That rippled whispering round her, came.
Her clear cold eyes, all glassy grey,
Seemed lit not with the light of day
But touched with gleams that waned away
 Of quelled and fading flame.

Before the king she bowed and spake:
"King, for thine old faith's plighted sake
To me the lady of the lake,
I come in trust of thee to take
 The guerdon of the gift I gave,
Thy sword Excalibur." And he
Made answer: "Be it whate'er it be,
If mine to give, I give it thee,
 Nor need is thine to crave."

As when a gleam of wicked light
Turns half a low-lying water bright
That moans beneath the shivering night
With sense of evil sound and sight
 And whispering witchcraft's bated breath,
Her wan face quickened as she said:
"This knight that won the sword—his head
I crave or hers that brought it. Dead,
 Let these be one in death."

"Not with mine honour this may be;
Ask all save this thou wilt," quoth he,
"And have thy full desire." But she
Made answer: "Nought will I of thee,
  Nought if not this." Then Balen turned,
And saw the sorceress hard beside
By whose fell craft his mother died:
Three years he had sought her, and here espied
  His heart against her yearned.

"Ill be thou met," he said, "whose ire
Would slake with blood thy soul's desire:
By thee my mother died in fire;
Die thou by me a death less dire."
  Sharp flashed his sword forth, fleet as flame,
And shore away her sorcerous head.
"Alas for shame," the high king said,
"That one found once my friend lies dead;
  Alas for all our shame!

"Thou shouldst have here forborne her; yea,
Were all the wrongs that bid men slay
Thine, heaped too high for wrath to weigh,
Not here before my face today
  Was thine the right to wreak thy wrong."
Still stood he then as one that found
His rose of hope by storm discrowned,
And all the joy that girt him round
  Brief as a broken song.

Yet ere he passed he turned and spake:
"King, only for thy nobler sake
Than aught of power man's power may take
Or pride of place that pride may break
  I bid the lordlier man in thee,
That lives within the king, give ear.
This justice done before thee here
On one that hell's own heart holds dear,
  Needs might not this but be.

"Albeit, for all that pride would prove,
My heart be wrung to lose thy love,
It yet repents me not hereof:
So many an eagle and many a dove,
  So many a knight, so many a may,
This water-snake of poisonous tongue
To death by words and wiles hath stung,
That her their slayer, from hell's lake sprung,

I did not ill to slay."

"Yea," said the king, "too high of heart
To stand before a king thou art;
Yet irks it me to bid thee part
And take thy penance for thy part,
    That God may put upon thy pride."
Then Balen took the severed head
And toward his hostry turned and sped
As one that knew not quick from dead
    Nor good from evil tide.

He bade his squire before him stand
And take that sanguine spoil in hand
And bear it far by shore and strand
Till all in glad Northumberland
    That loved him, seeing it, all might know
His deadliest foe was dead, and hear
How free from prison as from fear
He dwelt in trust of the answering year
    To bring him weal for woe.

"And tell them, now I take my way
To meet in battle, if I may,
King Ryons of North Wales, and slay
That king of kernes whose fiery sway
    Doth all the marches dire despite
That serve King Arthur: so shall he
Again be gracious lord to me,
And I that leave thee meet with thee
    Once more in Arthur's sight."

So spake he ere they parted, nor
Took shame or fear to counsellor,
As one whom none laid ambush for;
And wist not how Sir Launceor,
    The wild king's son of Ireland, hot
And high in wrath to know that one
Stood higher in fame before the sun,
Even Balen, since the sword was won,
    Drew nigh from Camelot.

For thence, in heat of hate and pride,
As one that man might bid not bide,
He craved the high king's grace to ride
On quest of Balen far and wide
    And wreak the wrong his wrath had wrought.
"Yea," Arthur said, "for such despite

Was done me never in my sight
As this thine hand shall now requite
  If trust avail us aught."

But ere he passed, in eager mood
To feed his hate with bitter food,
Before the king's face Merlin stood
And heard his tale of ill and good,
  Of Balen, and the sword achieved,
And whence it smote as heaven's red ire
That direful dame of doom as dire;
And how the king's wrath turned to fire
  The grief wherewith he grieved.

And darkening as he gave it ear,
The still face of the sacred seer
Waxed wan with wrath and not with fear,
And ever changed its cloudier cheer
  Till all his face was very night.
"This damosel that brought the sword,"
He said, "before the king my lord,
And all these knights about his board,
  Hath done them all despite.

"The falsest damosel she is
That works men ill on earth, I wis,
And all her mind is toward but this,
To kill as with a lying kiss
  Truth, and the life of noble trust.
A brother hath she,—see but now
The flame of shame that brands her brow!—
A true man, pure as faith's own vow,
  Whose honour knows not rust.

"This good knight found within her bower
A felon and her paramour,
And slew him in his shameful hour,
As right gave might and righteous power
  To hands that wreaked so foul a wrong.
Then, for the hate her heart put on,
She sought by ways where death had gone
The lady Lyle of Avalon,
  Whose crafts are strange and strong.

"The sorceress, one with her in thought,
Gave her that sword of magic, wrought
By charms whereof sweet heaven sees nought,
That hither girt on her she brought

To be by doom her brother's bane.
And grief it is to think how he
That won it, being of heart so free
And perfect found in chivalry,
   Shall by that sword lie slain.

Great pity it is and strange despite
That one whose eyes are stars to light
Honour, and shine as heaven's own height,
Should perish, being the goodliest knight
   That even the all-glorious north has borne.
Nor shall my lord the king behold
A lordlier friend of mightier mould
Than Balen, though his tale be told
   Ere noon fulfil his morn."

IV

As morning hears before it run
The music of the mounting sun,
And laughs to watch his trophies won
From darkness, and her hosts undone,
   And all the night become a breath,
Nor dreams that fear should hear and flee
The summer menace of the sea,
So hears our hope what life may be,
   And knows it not for death.

Each day that slays its hours and dies
Weeps, laughs, and lightens on our eyes,
And sees and hears not: smiles and sighs
As flowers ephemeral fall and rise
   About its birth, about its way,
And pass as love and sorrow pass,
As shadows flashing down a glass,
As dew-flowers blowing in flowerless grass,
   As hope from yesterday.

The blossom of the sunny dew
That now the stronger sun strikes through
Fades off the blade whereon it blew
No fleetlier than the flowers that grew
   On hope's green stem in life's fierce light.
Nor might the glory soon to sit
Awhile on Balen's crest alit
Outshine the shadow of doom on it
   Or stay death's wings from flight.

Dawn on a golden moorland side
By holt and heath saw Balen ride
And Launceor after, pricked with pride
And stung with spurring envy: wide
   And far he had ridden athwart strange lands
And sought amiss the man he found
And cried on, till the stormy sound
Rang as a rallying trumpet round
   That fires men's hearts and hands.

Abide he bade him: nor was need
To bid when Balen wheeled his steed
Fiercely, less fain by word than deed
To bid his envier evil speed,
   And cried, "What wilt thou with me?" Loud
Rang Launceor's vehement answer: "Knight,
To avenge on thee the dire despite
Thou hast done us all in Arthur's sight
   I stand toward Arthur vowed."

"Ay?" Balen said: "albeit I see
I needs must deal in strife with thee,
Light is the wyte thou layest on me;
For her I slew and sinned not, she
   Was dire in all men's eyes as death,
Or none were lother found than I
By me to bid a woman die:
As lief were loyal men to lie,
   Or scorn what honour saith."

As the arched wave's weight against the reef
Hurls, and is hurled back like a leaf
Storm-shrivelled, and its rage of grief
Speaks all the loud broad sea in brief,
   And quells the hearkening hearts of men,
Or as the crash of overfalls
Down under blue smooth water brawls
Like jarring steel on ruining walls,
   So rang their meeting then.

As wave on wave shocks, and confounds
The bounding bulk whereon it bounds
And breaks and shattering seaward sounds
As crying of the old sea's wolves and hounds
   That moan and ravin and rage and wail,
So steed on steed encountering sheer
Shocked, and the strength of Launceor's spear

Shivered on Balen's shield, and fear
  Bade hope within him quail.

But Balen's spear through Launceor's shield
Clove as a ploughshare cleaves the field
And pierced the hauberk triple-steeled,
That horse with horseman stricken reeled,
  And as a storm-breached rock falls, fell.
And Balen turned his horse again
And wist not yet his foe lay slain,
And saw him dead that sought his bane
  And wrought and fared not well.

Suddenly, while he gazed and stood,
And mused in many-minded mood
If life or death were evil or good,
Forth of a covert of a wood
  That skirted half the moorland lea
Fast rode a maiden flower-like white
Full toward that fair wild place of fight,
Anhungered of the woful sight
  God gave her there to see.

And seeing the man there fallen and dead,
She cried against the sun that shed
Light on the living world, and said,
"O Balen, slayer whose hand is red,
  Two bodies and one heart thou hast slain,
Two hearts within one body: aye,
Two souls thou hast lost; by thee they die,
Cast out of sight of earth and sky
  And all that made them fain."

And from the dead his sword she caught,
And fell in trance that wist of nought,
Swooning: but softly Balen sought
To win from her the sword she thought
  To die on, dying by Launceor's side.
Again her wakening wail outbroke
As wildly, sword in hand, she woke
And struck one swift and bitter stroke
  That healed her, and she died.

And sorrowing for their strange love's sake
Rode Balen forth by lawn and lake,
By moor and moss and briar and brake,
And in his heart their sorrow spake
  Whose lips were dumb as death, and said

Mute words of presage blind and vain
As rain-stars blurred and marred by rain
To wanderers on a moonless main
  Where night and day seem dead.

Then toward a sunbright wildwood side
He looked and saw beneath it ride
A knight whose arms afar espied
By note of name and proof of pride
  Bare witness of his brother born,
His brother Balan, hard at hand,
Twin flower of bright Northumberland,
Twin sea-bird of their loud sea-strand,
  Twin song-bird of their morn.

Ah then from Balen passed away
All dread of night, all doubt of day,
All care what life or death might say,
All thought of all worse months than May:
  Only the might of joy in love
Brake forth within him as a fire,
And deep delight in deep desire
Of far-flown days whose full-souled quire
  Rang round from the air above.

From choral earth and quiring air
Rang memories winged like songs that bear
Sweet gifts for spirit and sense to share:
For no man's life knows love more fair
  And fruitful of memorial things
Than this the deep dear love that breaks
With sense of life on life, and makes
The sundawn sunnier as it wakes
  Where morning round it rings.

"O brother, O my brother!" cried
Each upon each, and cast aside
Their helms unbraced that might not hide
From sight of memory single-eyed
  The likeness graven of face and face,
And kissed and wept upon each other
For joy and pity of either brother,
And love engrafted by sire and mother,
  God's natural gift of grace.

And each with each took counsel meet
For comfort, making sorrow sweet,
And grief a goodly thing to greet:

And word from word leapt light and fleet
  Till all the venturous tale was told,
And how in Balen's hope it lay
To meet the wild Welsh king and slay,
And win from Arthur back for pay
  The grace he gave of old.

"And thither will not thou with me
And win as great a grace for thee?"
"That will I well," quoth Balan: "we
Will cleave together, bound and free,
  As brethren should, being twain and one."
But ere they parted thence there came
A creature withered as with flame,
A dwarf mismade in nature's shame,
  Between them and the sun.

And riding fleet as fire may glide
He found the dead lie side by side,
And wailed and rent his hair and cried,
"Who hath done this deed?" And Balen eyed
  The strange thing loathfully, and said,
"The knight I slew, who found him fain
And keen to slay me: seeing him slain,
The maid I sought to save in vain,
  Self-stricken, here lies dead.

"Sore grief was mine to see her die,
And for her true faith's sake shall I
Love, and with love of heart more high,
All women better till I die."
  "Alas," the dwarf said, "ill for thee
In evil hour this deed was done:
For now the quest shall be begun
Against thee, from the dawning sun
  Even to the sunset sea.

"From shore to mountain, dawn to night,
The kinsfolk of this great dead knight
Will chase thee to thy death." A light
Of swift blithe scorn flashed answer bright
  As fire from Balen's eye. "For that,
Small fear shall fret my heart," quoth he:
"But that my lord the king should be
For this dead man's sake wroth with me,
  Weep might it well thereat."

Then murmuring passed the dwarf away,

And toward the knights in fair array
Came riding eastward up the way
From where the flower-soft lowlands lay
  A king whose name the sweet south-west
Held high in honour, and the land
That bowed beneath his gentle hand
Wore on its wild bright northern strand
  Tintagel for a crest.

And Balen hailed with homage due
King Mark of Cornwall, when he knew
The pennon that before him flew:
And for those lovers dead and true
  The king made moan to hear their doom;
And for their sorrow's sake he sware
To seek in all the marches there
The church that man might find most fair
  And build therein their tomb.

V

As thought from thought takes wing and flies,
As month on month with sunlit eyes
Tramples and triumphs in its rise,
As wave smites wave to death and dies,
  So chance on hurtling chance like steel
Strikes, flashes, and is quenched, ere fear
Can whisper hope, or hope can hear,
If sorrow or joy be far or near
  For time to hurt or heal.

Swift as a shadow and strange as light
That cleaves in twain the shadow of night
Before the wide-winged word takes flight
That thunder speaks to depth and height
  And quells the quiet hour with sound,
There came before King Mark and stood
Between the moorside and the wood
The man whose word God's will made good,
  Nor guile was in it found.

And Merlin said to Balen: "Lo,
Thou hast wrought thyself a grievous woe
To let this lady die, and know
Thou mightst have stayed her deadly blow."
  And Balen answered him and said,
"Nay, by my truth to faith, not I,

So fiercely fain she was to die;
Ere well her sword had flashed on high,
  Self-slain she lay there dead."

Again and sadly Merlin spake:
"My heart is wrung for this deed's sake,
To know thee therefore doomed to take
Upon thine hand a curse, and make
  Three kingdoms pine through twelve years' change,
In want and woe: for thou shalt smite
The man most noble and truest knight
That looks upon the live world's light
  A dolorous stroke and strange.

"And not till years shall round their goal
May this man's wound thou hast given be whole."
And Balen, stricken through the soul
By dark-winged words of doom and dole,
  Made answer: "If I wist it were
No lie but sooth thou sayest of me,
Then even to make a liar of thee
Would I too slay myself, and see
  How death bids dead men fare."

And Merlin took his leave and passed
And was not: and the shadow as fast
Went with him that his word had cast,
Too fleet for thought thereof to last:
  And there those brethren bade King Mark
Farewell: but fain would Mark have known
The strong knight's name who had overthrown
The pride of Launceor, when it shone
  Bright as it now lay dark.

And Balan for his brother spake,
Saying: "Sir, albeit him list not break
The seal of secret time, nor shake
Night off him ere his morning wake,
  By these two swords he is girt withal
May men that praise him, knights and lords,
Call him the knight that bears two swords,
And all the praise his fame accords
  Make answer when they call."

So parted they toward eventide;
And tender twilight, heavy-eyed,
Saw deep down glimmering woodlands ride
Balen and Balan side by side,

Till where the leaves grew dense and dim
Again they spied from far draw near
The presence of the sacred seer,
But so disguised and strange of cheer
  That seeing they knew not him.

"Now whither ride ye," Merlin said,
"Through shadows that the sun strikes red,
Ere night be born or day be dead?"
But they, for doubt half touched with dread,
  Would say not where their goal might lie.
"And thou," said Balen, "what art thou,
To walk with shrouded eye and brow?"
He said: "Me lists not show thee now
  By name what man am I."

"Ill seen is this of thee," said they,
"That thou art true in word and way
Nor fain to fear the face of day,
Who wilt not as a true man say
  The name it shames not him to bear."
He answered: "Be it or be it not so,
Yet why ye ride this way I know,
To meet King Ryons as a foe,
  And how your hope shall fare.

"Well, if ye hearken toward my rede,
Ill, if ye hear not, shall ye speed."
"Ah, now," they cried, "thou art ours at need
What Merlin saith we are fain to heed."
  "Great worship shall ye win," said he,
"And look that ye do knightly now,
For great shall be your need, I trow."
And Balen smiled: "By knighthood's vow,
  The best we may will we."

Then Merlin bade them turn and take
Rest, for their good steeds' weary sake,
Between the highway and the brake,
Till starry midnight bade them wake:
  Then "Rise," he said, "the king is nigh,
Who hath stolen from all his host away
With threescore horse in armed array,
The goodliest knights that bear his sway
  And hold his kingdom high.

"And twenty ride of them before
To bear his errand, ere the door

Turn of the night, sealed fast no more,
And sundawn bid the stars wax hoar;
  For by the starshine of to-night
He seeks a leman where she waits
His coming, dark and swift as fate's,
And hearkens toward the unopening gates
  That yield not him to sight.

Then through the glimmering gloom around
A shadowy sense of light and sound
Made, ere the proof thereof were found,
The brave blithe hearts within them bound,
  And "Where," quoth Balen, "rides the king?"
But softer spake the seer: "Abide,
Till hither toward your spears he ride,
Where all the narrowing woodland side
  Grows dense with boughs that cling."

There in that straitening way they met
The wild Welsh host against them set,
And smote their strong king down, ere yet
His hurrying horde of spears might get
  Fierce vantage of them. Then the fight
Grew great and joyous as it grew,
For left and right those brethren slew,
Till all the lawn waxed red with dew
  More deep than dews of night.

And ere the full fierce tale was read
Full forty lay before them dead,
And fast the hurtling remnant fled
And wist not whither fear had led:
  And toward the king they went again,
And would have slain him: but he bowed
Before them, crying in fear aloud
For grace they gave him, seeing the proud
  Wild king brought lowest of men.

And ere the wildwood leaves were stirred
With song or wing of wakening bird,
In Camelot was Merlin's word
With joy in joyous wonder heard
  That told of Arthur's bitterest foe
Diskingdomed and discomfited.
"By whom?" the high king smiled and said.
He answered: "Ere the dawn wax red,
  To-morrow bids you know.

"Two knights whose heart and hope are one
And fain to win your grace have done
This work whereby if grace be won
Their hearts shall hail the enkindling sun
    With joy more keen and deep than day."
And ere the sundawn drank the dew
Those brethren with their prisoner drew
To the outer guard they gave him to
    And passed again away.

And Arthur came as toward his guest
To greet his foe, and bade him rest
As one returned from nobler quest
And welcome from the stormbright west,
    But by what chance he fain would hear.
"The chance was hard and strange, sir king,"
Quoth Ryons, bowed in thanksgiving.
"Who won you?" Arthur said: "the thing
    Is worth a warrior's ear."

The wild king flushed with pride and shame,
Answering: "I know not either name
Of those that there against us came
And withered all our strength like flame:
    The knight that bears two swords is one,
And one his brother: not on earth
May men meet men of knightlier worth
Nor mightier born of mortal birth
    That hail the sovereign sun."

And Arthur said: "I know them not
But much am I for this, God wet,
Beholden to them: Launcelot
Nor Tristram, when the war waxed hot
    Along the marches east and west,
Wrought ever nobler work than this."
"Ah," Merlin said, "sore pity it is
And strange mischance of doom, I wis,
    That death should mar their quest.

"Balen, the perfect knight that won
The sword whose name is malison,
And made his deed his doom, is one:
Nor hath his brother Balan done
    Less royal service: not on earth
Lives there a nobler knight, more strong
Of soul to win men's praise in song,
Albeit the light abide not long

That lightened round his birth.

"Yea, and of all sad things I know
The heaviest and the highest in woe
Is this, the doom whose date brings low
Too soon in timeless overthrow
  A head so high, a hope so sure.
The greatest moan for any knight
That ever won fair fame in fight
Shall be for Balen, seeing his might
  Must now not long endure."

"Alas," King Arthur said, "he hath shown
Such love to me-ward that the moan
Made of him should be mine alone
Above all other, knowing it known
  I have ill deserved it of him." "Nay,"
Said Merlin, "he shall do for you
Much more, when time shall be anew,
Than time hath given him chance to do
  Or hope may think to say.

"But now must be your powers purveyed
To meet, ere noon of morn be made
To-morrow, all the host arrayed
Of this wild foe's wild brother, laid
  Around against you: see to it well,
For now I part from you." And soon,
When sundawn slew the withering moon,
Two hosts were met to win the boon
  Whose tale is death's to tell.

A lordly tale of knights and lords
For death to tell by count of swords
When war's wild harp in all its chords
Rang royal triumph, and the hordes
  Of hurtling foemen rocked and reeled
As waves wind-thwarted on the sea,
Was told of all that there might be,
Till scarce might battle hear or see
  The fortune of the field.

And many a knight won fame that day
When even the serpent soul of Kay
Was kindled toward the fiery play
As might a lion's be for prey,
  And won him fame that might not die
With passing of his rancorous breath

But clung about his life and death
As fire that speaks in cloud, and saith
   What strong men hear and fly.

And glorious works were Arthur's there,
That lit the battle-darkened air:
But when they saw before them fare
Like stars of storm the knight that bare
   Two swords about him girt for fray,
Balen, and Balan with him, then
Strong wonder smote the souls of men
If heaven's own host or hell's deep den
   Had sent them forth to slay.

So keen they rode across the fight,
So sharp they smote to left and right,
And made of hurtling darkness light
With lightning of their swords, till flight
   And fear before them flew like flame,
That Arthur's self had never known,
He said, since first his blast was blown,
Such lords of war as these alone
   That whence he knew not came.

But while the fire of war waxed hot
The wild king hearkened, hearing not,
Through storm of spears and arrow-shot,
For succour toward him from King Lot
   And all his host of sea-born men,
Strong as the strong storm-baffling bird
Whose cry round Orkney's headlands heard
Is as the sea's own sovereign word
   That mocks our mortal ken.

For Merlin's craft of prophecy,
Who wist that one of twain must die,
Put might in him to say thereby
Which head should lose its crown, and lie
   Stricken, though loth he were to know
That either life should wane and fail;
Yet most might Arthur's love avail,
And still with subtly tempered tale
   His wile held fast the foe.

With woven words of magic might
Wherein the subtle shadow and light
Changed hope and fear till fear took flight,
He stayed King Lot's fierce lust of fight

Till all the wild Welsh war was driven
As foam before the wind that wakes
With the all-awakening sun, and breaks
Strong ships that rue the mirth it makes
   When grace to slay is given.

And ever hotter lit and higher,
As fire that meets encountering fire,
Waxed in King Lot his keen desire
To bid revenge within him tire
   On Arthur's ravaged fame and life:
Across the waves of war between
Floated and flashed, unseen and seen,
The lustrous likeness of the queen
   Whom shame had sealed his wife.

But when the woful word was brought
That while he tarried, doubting nought,
The hope was lost whose goal he sought
And all the fight he yearned for fought,
   His heart was rent for grief and shame,
And half his hope was set on flight
Till word was given him of a knight
Who said: "They are weary and worn with fight,
   And we more fresh than flame."

And bright and dark as night and day
Ere either find the unopening way
Clear, and forego the unaltering sway,
The sad king's face shone, frowning: "Yea,
   I would that every knight of mine
Would do his part as I shall do,"
He said, "till death or life anew
Shall judge between us as is due
   With wiser doom than thine."

Then thundered all the awakening field
With crash of hosts that clashed and reeled,
Banner to banner, shield to shield,
And spear to splintering spear-shaft, steeled
   As heart against high heart of man,
As hope against high hope of knight
To pluck the crest and crown of fight
From war's clenched hand by storm's wild light,
   For blessing given or ban.

All hearts of hearkening men that heard
The ban twin-born with blessing, stirred

Like springtide waters, knew the word
Whereby the steeds of storm are spurred
  With ravenous rapture to destroy,
And laughed for love of battle, pierced
With passion of tempestuous thirst
And hungering hope to assuage it first
  With draughts of stormy joy.

But sheer ahead of the iron tide
That rocked and roared from side to side
Rode as the lightning's lord might ride
King Lot, whose heart was set to abide
  All peril of the raging hour,
And all his host of warriors born
Where lands by warring seas are worn
Was only by his hands upborne
  Who gave them pride and power.

But as the sea's hand smites the shore
And shatters all the strengths that bore
The ravage earth may bear no more,
So smote the hand of Pellinore
  Charging, a knight of Arthur's chief,
And clove his strong steed's neck in twain,
And smote him sheer through brow and brain,
Falling: and there King Lot lay slain,
  And knew not wrath or grief.

And all the host of Orkney fled,
And many a mother's son lay dead:
But when they raised the stricken head
Whence pride and power and shame were fled
  And rage and anguish now cast out,
And bore it toward a kingly tomb,
The wife whose love had wrought his doom
Came thither, fair as morning's bloom
  And dark as twilight's doubt.

And there her four strong sons and his,
Gawain and Gareth, Gaherys
And Agravain, whose sword's sharp kiss
With sound of hell's own serpent's hiss
  Should one day turn her life to death,
Stood mourning with her: but by these
Seeing Mordred as a seer that sees,
Anguish of terror bent her knees
  And caught her shuddering breath.

The splendour of her sovereign eyes
Flashed darkness deeper than the skies
Feel or fear when the sunset dies
On his that felt as midnight rise
    Their doom upon them, there undone
By faith in fear ere thought could yield
A shadowy sense of days revealed,
The ravin of the final field,
    The terror of their son.

For Arthur's, as they caught the light
That sought and durst not seek his sight,
Darkened, and all his spirit's might
Withered within him even as night
    Withers when sunrise thrills the sea.
But Mordred's lightened as with fire
That smote his mother and his sire
With darkling doom and deep desire
    That bade its darkness be.

And heavier on their hearts the weight
Sank of the fear that brings forth fate,
The bitter doubt whose womb is great
With all the grief and love and hate
    That turn to fire men's days on earth.
And glorious was the funeral made,
And dark the deepening dread that swayed
Their darkening souls whose light grew shade
    With sense of death in birth.

VI

In autumn, when the wind and sea
Rejoice to live and laugh to be,
And scarce the blast that curbs the tree
And bids before it quail and flee
    The fiery foliage, where its brand
Is radiant as the seal of spring,
Sounds less delight, and waves a wing
Less lustrous, life's loud thanksgiving
    Puts life in sea and land.

High hope in Balen's heart alight
Laughed, as from all that clamorous fight
He passed and sought not Arthur's sight,
Who fain had found his kingliest knight
    And made amend for Balen's wrong.

But Merlin gave his soul to see
Fate, rising as a shoreward sea,
And all the sorrow that should be
   Ere hope or fear thought long.

"O where are they whose hands upbore
My battle," Arthur said, "before
The wild Welsh host's wide rage and roar?
Balen and Balan, Pellinore,
   Where are they?" Merlin answered him:
"Balen shall be not long away
From sight of you, but night nor day
Shall bring his brother back to say
   If life burn bright or dim."

"Now, by my faith," said Arthur then,
"Two marvellous knights are they, whose ken
Toward battle makes the twain as ten,
And Balen most of all born men
   Passeth of prowess all I know
Or ever found or sought to see:
Would God he would abide with me,
To face the times foretold of thee
   And all the latter woe."

For there had Merlin shown the king
The doom that songs unborn should sing,
The gifts that time should rise and bring
Of blithe and bitter days to spring
   As weeds and flowers against the sun.
And on the king for fear's sake fell
Sickness, and sorrow deep as hell,
Nor even might sleep bid fear farewell
   If grace to sleep were won.

Down in a meadow green and still
He bade the folk that wrought his will
Pitch his pavilion, where the chill
Soft night would let not rest fulfil
   His heart wherein dark fears lay deep.
And sharp against his hearing cast
Came a sound as of horsehoofs fast
Passing, that ere their sound were past
   Aroused him as from sleep.

And forth he looked along the grass
And saw before his portal pass
A knight that wailed aloud, "Alas

That life should find this dolorous pass
    And find no shield from doom and dole!"
And hearing all his moan, "Abide,
Fair sir," the king arose and cried,
"And say what sorrow bids you ride
    So sorrowful of soul."

"My hurt may no man heal, God wot,
And help of man may speed me not,"
The sad knight said, "nor change my lot."
And toward the castle of Melyot
    Whose towers arose a league away
He passed forth sorrowing: and anon,
Ere well the woful sight were gone,
Came Balen down the meads that shone,
    Strong, bright, and brave as day.

And seeing the king there stand, the knight
Drew rein before his face to alight
In reverence made for love's sake bright
With joy that set his face alight
    As theirs who see, alive, above,
The sovereign of their souls, whose name
To them is even as love's own flame
To enkindle hope that heeds not fame
    And knows no lord but love.

And Arthur smiled on him, and said,
"Right welcome be thou: by my head,
I would not wish me better sped.
For even but now there came and fled
    Before me like a cloud that flies
A knight that made most heavy cheer,
I know not wherefore; nor may fear
Or pity give my heart to hear
    Or lighten on mine eyes.

"But even for fear's and pity's sake
Fain were I thou shouldst overtake
And fetch again this knight that spake
No word of answering grace to make
    Reply to mine that hailed him: thou,
By force or by goodwill, shalt bring
His face before me." "Yea, my king,"
Quoth Balen, "and a greater thing
    Were less than is my vow.

"I would the task required and heard

Were heavier than your sovereign word
Hath laid on me:" and thence he spurred
Elate at heart as youth, and stirred
  With hope as blithe as fires a boy:
And many a mile he rode, and found
Far in a forest's glimmering bound
The man he sought afar around
  And seeing took fire for joy.

And with him went a maiden, fair
As flowers aflush with April air.
And Balen bade him turn him there
To tell the king what woes they were
  That bowed him down so sore: and he
Made woeful answer: "This should do
Great scathe to me, with nought for you
Of help that hope might hearken to
  For boot that may not be."

And Balen answered: "I were loth
To fight as one perforce made wroth
With one that owes by knighthood's oath
One love, one service, and one troth
  With me to him whose gracious hand
Holds fast the helm of knighthood here
Whereby man's hope and heart may steer:
I pray you let not sorrow or fear
  Against his bidding stand."

The strange knight gazed on him, and spake:
"Will you, for Arthur's royal sake,
Be warrant for me that I take
No scathe from strife that man may make?
  Then will I go with you." And he
Made joyous answer: "Yea, for I
Will be your warrant or will die."
And thence they rode with hearts as high
  As men's that search the sea.

And as by noon's large light the twain
Before the tented hall drew rein,
Suddenly fell the strange knight, slain
By one that came and went again
  And none might see him; but his spear
Clove through the body, swift as fire,
The man whose doom, forefelt as dire,
Had darkened all his life's desire,
  As one that death held dear.

And dying he turned his face and said,
"Lo now thy warrant that my head
Should fall not, following forth where led
A knight whose pledge hath left me dead.
    This darkling manslayer hath to name
Garlon: take thou my goodlier steed,
Seeing thine is less of strength and speed,
And ride, if thou be knight indeed,
    Even thither whence we came.

"And as the maiden's fair behest
Shall bid you follow on my quest,
Follow: and when God's will sees best,
Revenge my death, and let me rest
    As one that lived and died a knight,
Unstained of shame alive or dead."
And Balen, wrung with sorrow, said,
"That shall I do: my hand and head
    I pledge to do you right."

And thence with sorrowing heart and cheer
He rode, in grief that cast out fear
Lest death in darkness yet were near,
And bore the truncheon of the spear
    Wherewith the woful knight lay slain
To her with whom he rode, and she
Still bare it with her, fain to see
What righteous doom of God's might be
    The darkling manslayer's bane.

And down a dim deep woodland way
They rode between the boughs asway
With flickering winds whose flash and play
Made sunlight sunnier where the day
    Laughed, leapt, and fluttered like a bird
Caught in a light loose leafy net
That earth for amorous heaven had set
To hold and see the sundawn yet
    And hear what morning heard.

There in the sweet soft shifting light
Across their passage rode a knight
Flushed hot from hunting as from fight,
And seeing the sorrow-stricken sight
    Made question of them why they rode
As mourners sick at heart and sad,
When all alive about them bade

Sweet earth for heaven's sweet sake be glad
  As heaven for earth's love glowed.

"Me lists not tell you," Balen said.
The strange knight's face grew keen and red
"Now, might my hand but keep my head,
Even here should one of twain lie dead
  Were he no better armed than I."
And Balen spake with smiling speed,
Where scorn and courtesy kept heed
Of either: "That should little need:
  Not here shall either die."

And all the cause he told him through
As one that feared not though he knew
All: and the strange knight spake anew,
Saying: "I will part no more from you
  While life shall last me." So they went
Where he might arm himself to ride,
And rode across wild ways and wide
To where against a churchyard side
  A hermit's harbour leant.

And there against them riding came
Fleet as the lightning's laugh and flame
The invisible evil, even the same
They sought and might not curse by name
  As hell's foul child on earth set free,
And smote the strange knight through, and fled,
And left the mourners by the dead.
"Alas, again," Sir Balen said,
  "This wrong he hath done to me."

And there they laid their dead to sleep
Royally, lying where wild winds keep
Keen watch and wail more soft and deep
Than where men's choirs bid music weep
  And song like incense heave and swell.
And forth again they rode, and found
Before them, dire in sight and sound,
A castle girt about and bound
  With sorrow like a spell.

Above it seemed the sun at noon
Sad as a wintry withering moon
That shudders while the waste wind's tune
Craves ever none may guess what boon,
  But all may know the boon for dire.

And evening on its darkness fell
More dark than very death's farewell,
And night about it hung like hell,
  Whose fume the dawn made fire.

And Balen lighted down and passed
Within the gateway, whence no blast
Rang as the sheer portcullis, cast
Suddenly down, fell, and made fast
  The gate behind him, whence he spied
A sudden rage of men without
And ravin of a murderous rout
That girt the maiden hard about
  With death on either side.

And seeing that shame and peril, fear
Bade wrath and grief awake and hear
What shame should say in fame's wide ear
If she, by sorrow sealed more dear
  Than joy might make her, so should die:
And up the tower's curled stair he sprang
As one that flies death's deadliest fang,
And leapt right out amid their gang
  As fire from heaven on high.

And they thereunder seeing the knight
Unhurt among their press alight
And bare his sword for chance of fight
Stood from him, loth to strive or smite,
  And bade him hear their woful word,
That not the maiden's death they sought;
But there through years too dire for thought
Had lain their lady stricken, and nought
  Might heal her: and he heard.

For there a maiden clean and whole
In virgin body and virgin soul,
Whose name was writ on royal roll,
That would but stain a silver bowl
  With offering of her stainless blood,
Therewith might heal her: so they stayed
For hope's sad sake each blameless maid
There journeying in that dolorous shade
  Whose bloom was bright in bud.

No hurt nor harm to her it were
If she should yield a sister there
Some tribute of her blood, and fare

Forth with this joy at heart to bear,
　That all unhurt and unafraid
This grace she had here by God's grace wrought.
And kindling all with kindly thought
And love that saw save love's self nought,
　Shone, smiled, and spake the maid.

"Good knight of mine, good will have I
To help this healing though I die."
"Nay," Balen said, "but love may try
What help in living love may lie.
　—I will not lose the life of her
While my life lasteth." So she gave
The tribute love was fain to crave,
But might not heal though fain to save,
　Were God's grace helpfuller.

Another maid in later Mays
Won with her life that woful praise,
And died. But they, when surging day's
Deep tide fulfilled the dawn's wide ways,
　Rode forth, and found by day or night
No chance to cross their wayfaring
Till when they saw the fourth day spring
A knight's hall gave them harbouring
　Rich as a king's house might.

And while they sat at meat and spake
Words bright and kind as grace might make
Sweet for true knighthood's kindly sake,
They heard a cry beside them break
　The still-souled joy of blameless rest.
"What noise is this?" quoth Balen. "Nay,"
His knightly host made answer, "may
Our grief not grieve you though I say
　How here I dwell unblest.

"Not many a day has lived and died
Since at a tournay late I tried
My strength to smite and turn and ride
Against a knight of kinglike pride,
　King Pellam's brother: twice I smote
The splendour of his strength to dust:
And he, fulfilled of hate's fierce lust,
Swore vengeance, pledged for hell to trust,
　And keen as hell's wide throat.

"Invisible as the spirit of night

That heaven and earth in depth and height
May see not by the mild moon's light
Nor even when stars would grant them sight,
　He walks and slays as plague's blind breath
Slays: and my son, whose anguish here
Makes moan perforce that mars our cheer,
He wounded, even ere love might fear
　That hate were strong as death.

"Nor may my son be whole till he
Whose stroke through him hath stricken me
Shall give again his blood to be
Our healing: yet may no man see
　This felon, clothed with darkness round
And keen as lightning's life." Thereon
Spake Balen, and his presence shone
Even as the sun's when stars are gone
　That hear dawn's trumpet sound.

"That knight I know: two knights of mine,
Two comrades, sealed by faith's bright sign,
Whose eyes as ours that live should shine,
And drink the golden sunlight's wine
　With joy's thanksgiving that they live,
He hath slain in even the same blind wise:
Were all wide wealth beneath the skies
Mine, might I meet him, eyes on eyes,
　All would I laugh to give."

His host made answer, and his gaze
Grew bright with trust as dawn's moist maze
With fire: "Within these twenty days,
King Pellam, lord of Lystenayse,
　Holds feast through all this country cried,
And there before the knightly king
May no knight come except he bring
For witness of his wayfaring
　His paramour or bride.

"And there that day, so soon to shine,
This knight, your felon foe and mine,
Shall show, full-flushed with bloodred wine,
The fierce false face whereon we pine
　To wreak the wrong he hath wrought us, bare
As shame should see and brand it." "Then,"
Said Balen, "shall he give again
His blood to heal your son, and men
　Shall see death blind him there."

"Forth will we fare to-morrow," said
His host: and forth, as sunrise led,
They rode; and fifteen days were fled
Ere toward their goal their steeds had sped.
    And there alighting might they find
For Balen's host no place to rest,
Who came without a gentler guest
Beside him: and that household's hest
    Bade leave his sword behind.

"Nay," Balen said, "that do I not:
My country's custom stands, God wot,
That none whose lot is knighthood's lot,
To ride where chance as fire is hot
    With hope or promise given of fight,
Shall fail to keep, for knighthood's part,
His weapon with him as his heart;
And as I came will I depart,
    Or hold herein my right."

Then gat he leave to wear his sword
Beside the strange king's festal board
Where feasted many a knight and lord
In seemliness of fair accord:
    And Balen asked of one beside,
"Is there not in this court, if fame
Keep faith, a knight that hath to name
Garlon?" and saying that word of shame,
    He scanned that place of pride.

"Yonder he goeth against the light,
He with the face as swart as night,"
Quoth the other: "but he rides to fight
Hid round by charms from all men's sight,
    And many a noble knight he hath slain,
Being wrapt in darkness deep as hell
And silence dark as shame." "Ah, well,"
Said Balen, "is that he? the spell
    May be the sorcerer's bane."

Then Balen gazed upon him long,
And thought, "If here I wreak my wrong,
Alive I may not scape, so strong
The felon's friends about him throng;
    And if I leave him here alive,
This chance perchance may life not give
Again: much evil, if he live,

He needs must do, should fear forgive
  When wrongs bid strike and strive."

And Garlon, seeing how Balen's eye
Dwelt on him as his heart waxed high
With joy in wrath to see him nigh,
Rose wolf-like with a wolfish cry
  And crossed and smote him on the face,
Saying, "Knight, what wouldst thou with me? Eat,
For shame, and gaze not: eat thy meat
Do that thou art come for: stands thy seat
  Next ours of royal race?"

"Well hast thou said: thy rede rings true;
That which I came for will I do,"
Quoth Balen: forth his fleet sword flew,
And clove the head of Garlon through
  Clean to the shoulders. Then he cried
Loud to his lady, "Give me here
The truncheon of the shameful spear
Wherewith he slew your knight, when fear
  Bade hate in darkness ride."

And gladly, bright with grief made glad,
She gave the truncheon as he bade,
For still she bare it with her, sad
And strong in hopeless hope she had,
  Through all dark days of thwarting fear,
To see if doom should fall aright
And as God's fire-fraught thunder smite
That head, clothed round with hell-faced night,
  Bare now before her here.

And Balen smote therewith the dead
Dark felon's body through, and said
Aloud, "With even this truncheon, red
With baser blood than brave men bled
  Whom in thy shameful hand it slew,
Thou hast slain a nobler knight, and now
It clings and cleaves thy body: thou
Shall cleave again no brave man's brow,
  Though hell would aid anew."

And toward his host he turned and spake;
"Now for your son's long-suffering sake
Blood ye may fetch enough, and take
Wherewith to heal his hurt, and make
  Death warm as life." Then rose a cry

Loud as the wind's when stormy spring
Makes all the woodland rage and ring:
"Thou hast slain my brother," said the king,
  "And here with him shalt die."

"Ay?" Balen laughed him answer. "Well,
Do it then thyself." And the answer fell
Fierce as a blast of hate from hell,
"No man of mine that with me dwell
  Shall strike at thee but I their lord
For love of this my brother slain."
And Pellam caught and grasped amain
A grim great weapon, fierce and fain
  To feed his hungering sword.

And eagerly he smote, and sped
Not well: for Balen's blade, yet red
With lifeblood of the murderous dead,
Between the swordstroke and his head
  Shone, and the strength of the eager stroke
Shore it in sunder: then the knight,
Naked and weaponless for fight,
Ran seeking him a sword to smite
  As hope within him woke.

And so their flight for deathward fast
From chamber forth to chamber passed
Where lay no weapon, till the last
Whose doors made way for Balen cast
  Upon him as a sudden spell
Wonder that even as lightning leapt
Across his heart and eyes, and swept
As storm across his soul that kept
  Wild watch, and watched not well.

For there the deed he did, being near
Death's danger, breathless as the deer
Driven hard to bay, but void of fear,
Brought sorrow down for many a year
  On many a man in many a land.
All glorious shone that chamber, bright
As burns at sunrise heaven's own height:
With cloth of gold the bed was dight,
  That flamed on either hand.

And one he saw within it lie:
A table of all clear gold thereby
Stood stately, fair as morning's eye,

With four strong silver pillars, high
  And firm as faith and hope may be:
And on it shone the gift he sought,
A spear most marvellously wrought,
That when his eye and handgrip caught
  Small fear at heart had he.

Right on King Pellam then, as fire
Turns when the thwarting winds wax higher,
He turned, and smote him down. So dire
The stroke was, when his heart's desire
  Struck, and had all its fill of hate,
That as the king fell swooning down
Fell the walls, rent from base to crown,
Prone as prone seas that break and drown
  Ships fraught with doom for freight.

And there for three days' silent space
Balen and Pellam face to face
Lay dead or deathlike, and the place
Was death's blind kingdom, till the grace
  That God had given the sacred seer
For counsel or for comfort led
His Merlin thither, and he said,
Standing between the quick and dead,
  "Rise up, and rest not here."

And Balen rose and set his eyes
Against the seer's as one that tries
His heart against the sea's and sky's
And fears not if he lives or dies,
  Saying, "I would have my damosel,
Ere I fare forth, to fare with me."
And sadly Merlin answered, "See
Where now she lies; death knows if she
  Shall now fare ill or well.

"And in this world we meet no more,
Balen." And Balen, sorrowing sore,
Though fearless yet the heart he bore
Beat toward the life that lay before,
  Rode forth through many a wild waste land
Where men cried out against him, mad
With grievous faith in fear that bade
Their wrath make moan for doubt they had
  Lest hell had armed his hand.

For in that chamber's wondrous shrine

Was part of Christ's own blood, the wine
Shed of the true triumphal vine
Whose growth bids earth's deep darkness shine
  As heaven's deep light through the air and sea;
That mystery toward our northern shore
Arimathean Joseph bore
For healing of our sins of yore,
  That grace even there might be.

And with that spear there shrined apart
Was Christ's side smitten to the heart.
And fiercer than the lightning's dart
The stroke was, and the deathlike smart
  Wherewith, nigh drained of blood and breath,
The king lay stricken as one long dead:
And Joseph's was the blood there shed,
For near akin was he that bled,
  Near even as life to death.

And therefore fell on all that land
Sorrow: for still on either hand,
As Balen rode alone and scanned
Bright fields and cities built to stand
  Till time should break them, dead men lay;
And loud and long from all their folk
Living, one cry that cursed him broke;
Three countries had his dolorous stroke
  Slain, or should surely slay.

VII

In winter, when the year burns low
As fire wherein no firebrands glow,
And winds dishevel as they blow
The lovely stormy wings of snow,
  The hearts of northern men burn bright
With joy that mocks the joy of spring
To hear all heaven's keen clarions ring
Music that bids the spirit sing
  And day give thanks for night.

Aloud and dark as hell or hate
Round Balen's head the wind of fate
Blew storm and cloud from death's wide gate:
But joy as grief in him was great
  To face God's doom and live or die,
Sorrowing for ill wrought unaware,

Rejoicing in desire to dare
All ill that innocence might bear
  With changeless heart and eye.

Yet passing fain he was when past
Those lands and woes at length and last.
Eight times, as thence he fared forth fast,
Dawn rose and even was overcast
  With starry darkness dear as day,
Before his venturous quest might meet
Adventure, seeing within a sweet
Green low-lying forest, hushed in heat,
  A tower that barred his way.

Strong summer, dumb with rapture, bound
With golden calm the woodlands round
Wherethrough the knight forth faring found
A knight that on the greenwood ground
  Sat mourning: fair he was to see,
And moulded as for love or fight
A maiden's dreams might frame her knight;
But sad in joy's far-flowering sight
  As grief's blind thrall might be.

"God save you," Balen softly said,
"What grief bows down your heart and head
Thus, as one sorrowing for his dead?
Tell me, if haply I may stead
  In aught your sorrow, that I may."
"Sir knight," that other said, "thy word
Makes my grief heavier that I heard."
And pity and wonder inly stirred
  Drew Balen thence away.

And so withdrawn with silent speed
He saw the sad knight's stately steed,
A war-horse meet for warrior's need,
That none who passed might choose but heed,
  So strong he stood, so great, so fair,
With eyes afire for flight or fight,
A joy to look on, mild in might,
And swift and keen and kind as light,
  And all as clear of care.

And Balen, gazing on him, heard
Again his master's woful word
Sound sorrow through the calm unstirred
By fluttering wind or flickering bird,

Thus: "Ah, fair lady and faithless, why
Break thy pledged faith to meet me? soon
An hour beyond thy trothplight noon
Shall strike my death-bell, and thy boon
  Is this, that here I die.

"My curse for all thy gifts may be
Heavier than death or night on thee;
For now this sword thou gavest me
Shall set me from thy bondage free."
  And there the man had died self-slain,
But Balen leapt on him and caught
The blind fierce hand that fain had wrought
Self-murder, stung with fire of thought,
  As rage makes anguish fain.

Then, mad for thwarted grief, "Let go
My hand," the fool of wrath and woe
Cried, "or I slay thee." Scarce the glow
In Balen's cheek and eye might show,
  As dawn shows day while seas lie chill,
He heard, though pity took not heed,
But smiled and spake, "That shall not need:
What man may do to bid you speed
  I, so God speed me, will."

And the other craved his name, beguiled
By hope that made his madness mild.
Again Sir Balen spake and smiled:
"My name is Balen, called the Wild
  By knights whom kings and courts make tame
Because I ride alone afar
And follow but my soul for star."
"Ah, sir, I know the knight you are
  And all your fiery fame.

"The knight that bears two swords I know,
Most praised of all men, friend and foe,
For prowess of your hands, that show
Dark war the way where balefires glow
  And kindle glory like the dawn's."
So spake the sorrowing knight, and stood
As one whose heart fresh hope made good:
And forth they rode by wold and wood
  And down the glimmering lawns.

And Balen craved his name who rode
Beside him, where the wild wood glowed

With joy to feel how noontide flowed
Through glade and glen and rough green road
    Till earth grew joyful as the sea.
"My name is Garnysshe of the Mount,
A poor man's son of none account,"
He said, "where springs of loftier fount
    Laugh loud with pride to be.

"But strength in weakness lives and stands
As rocks that rise through shifting sands;
And for the prowess of my hands
One made me knight and gave me lands,
    Duke Hermel, lord from far to near,
Our prince; and she that loved me—she
I love, and deemed she loved but me,
His daughter, pledged her faith to be
    Ere now beside me here."

And Balen, brief of speech as light
Whose word, beheld of depth and height,
Strikes silence through the stars of night,
Spake, and his face as dawn's grew bright,
    For hope to help a happier man,
"How far then lies she hence?" "By this,"
Her lover sighed and said, "I wis,
Not six fleet miles the passage is,
    And straight as thought could span."

So rode they swift and sure, and found
A castle walled and dyked around:
And Balen, as a warrior bound
On search where hope might fear to sound
    The darkness of the deeps of doubt,
Made entrance through the guardless gate
As life, while hope in life grows great,
Makes way between the doors of fate
    That death may pass thereout.

Through many a glorious chamber, wrought
For all delight that love's own thought
Might dream or dwell in, Balen sought
And found of all he looked for nought,
    For like a shining shell her bed
Shone void and vacant of her: thence
Through devious wonders bright and dense
He passed and saw with shame-struck sense
    Where shame and faith lay dead.

Down in a sweet small garden, fair
With flowerful joy in the ardent air,
He saw, and raged with loathing, where
She lay with love-dishevelled hair
   Beneath a broad bright laurel tree
And clasped in amorous arms a knight,
The unloveliest that his scornful sight
Had dwelt on yet; a shame the bright
   Broad noon might shrink to see.

And thence in wrathful hope he turned,
Hot as the heart within him burned,
To meet the knight whose love, so spurned
And spat on and made nought of, yearned
   And dreamed and hoped and lived in vain,
And said, "I have found her sleeping fast,"
And led him where the shadows cast
From leaves wherethrough light winds ran past
   Screened her from sun and rain.

But Garnysshe, seeing, reeled as he stood
Like a tree, kingliest of the wood,
Half hewn through: and the burning blood
Through lips and nostrils burst aflood:
   And gathering back his rage and might
As broken breakers rally and roar
The loud wind down that drives off shore,
He smote their heads off: there no more
   Their life might shame the light.

Then turned he back toward Balen, mad
With grief, and said, "The grief I had
Was nought: ere this my life was glad:
Thou hast done this deed: I was but sad
   And fearful how my hope might fare:
I had lived my sorrow down, hadst thou
Not shown me what I saw but now."
The sorrow and scorn on Balen's brow
   Bade silence curb him there.

And Balen answered: "What I did
I did to hearten thee and bid
Thy courage know that shame should rid
A man's high heart of love that hid
   Blind shame within its core: God knows,
I did, to set a bondman free,
But as I would thou hadst done by me,
That seeing what love must die to see

Love's end might well be woe's."

"Alas," the woful weakling said,
"I have slain what most I loved: I have shed
The blood most near my heart: the head
Lies cold as earth, defiled and dead,
   That all my life was lighted by,
That all my soul bowed down before,
And now may bear with life no more:
For now my sorrow that I bore
   Is twofold, and I die."

Then with his red wet sword he rove
His breast in sunder, where it clove
Life, and no pulse against it strove,
So sure and strong the deep stroke drove
   Deathward: and Balen, seeing him dead,
Rode thence, lest folk would say he had slain
Those three; and ere three days again
Had seen the sun's might wax and wane,
   Far forth he had spurred and sped.

And riding past a cross whereon
Broad golden letters written shone,
Saying, "No knight born may ride alone
Forth toward this castle," and all the stone
   Glowed in the sun's glare even as though
Blood stained it from the crucified
Dead burden of one that there had died,
An old hoar man he saw beside
   Whose face was wan as woe.

"Balen the Wild," he said, "this way
Thy way lies not: thou hast passed to-day
Thy bands: but turn again, and stay
Thy passage, while thy soul hath sway
   Within thee, and through God's good power
It will avail thee:" and anon
His likeness as a cloud was gone,
And Balen's heart within him shone
   Clear as the cloudless hour.

Nor fate nor fear might overcast
The soul now near its peace at last.
Suddenly, thence as forth he past,
A mighty and a deadly blast
   Blown of a hunting-horn he heard,
As when the chase hath nobly sped.

"That blast is blown for me," he said,
"The prize am I who am yet not dead,"
  And smiled upon the word.

As toward a royal hart's death rang
That note, whence all the loud wood sang
With winged and living sound that sprang
Like fire, and keen as fire's own fang
  Pierced the sweet silence that it slew.
But nought like death or strife was here:
Fair semblance and most goodly cheer
They made him, they whose troop drew near
  As death among them drew.

A hundred ladies well arrayed
And many a knight well weaponed made
That kindly show of cheer: the glade
Shone round them till its very shade
  Lightened and laughed from grove to lawn
To hear and see them: so they brought
Within a castle fair as thought
Could dream that wizard hands had wrought
  The guest among them drawn.

All manner of glorious joy was there:
Harping and dancing, loud and fair,
And minstrelsy that made of air
Fire, so like fire its raptures were.
  Then the chief lady spake on high:
"Knight with the two swords, one of two
Must help you here or fall from you:
For needs you now must have ado
  And joust with one hereby.

"A good knight guards an island here
Against all swords that chance brings near,
And there with stroke of sword and spear
Must all for whom these halls make cheer
  Fight, and redeem or yield up life."
"An evil custom," Balen said,
"Is this, that none whom chance hath led
Hither, if knighthood crown his head,
  May pass unstirred to strife."

"You shall not have ado to fight
Here save against one only knight,"
She said, and all her face grew bright
As hell-fire, lit with hungry light

That wicked laughter touched with flame.
"Well, since I shall thereto," said he,
"I am ready at heart as death for me:
Fain would I be where death should be
   And life should lose its name.

"But travelling men whose goal afar
Shines as a cloud-constraining star
Are often weary, and wearier are
Their steeds that feel each fret and jar
   Wherewith the wild ways wound them: yet,
Albeit my horse be weary, still
My heart is nowise weary; will
Sustains it even till death fulfil
   My trust upon him set."

"Sir," said a knight thereby that stood,
"Meseems your shield is now not good
But worn with warrior work, nor could
Sustain in strife the strokes it would:
   A larger will I lend you." "Ay,
Thereof I thank you," Balen said,
Being single of heart as one that read
No face aright whence faith had fled,
   Nor dreamed that faith could fly.

And so he took that shield unknown
And left for treason's touch his own,
And toward that island rode alone,
Nor heard the blast against him blown
   Sound in the wind's and water's sound,
But hearkening toward the stream's edge heard
Nought save the soft stream's rippling word,
Glad with the gladness of a bird,
   That sang to the air around.

And there against the water-side
He saw, fast moored to rock and ride,
A fair great boat anear abide
Like one that waits the turning tide,
   Wherein embarked his horse and he
Passed over toward no kindly strand:
And where they stood again on land
There stood a maiden hard at hand
   Who seeing them wept to see.

And "O knight Balen," was her cry,
"Why have ye left your own shield? why

Come hither out of time to die?
For had ye kept your shield, thereby
　Ye had yet been known, and died not here.
Great pity it is of you this day
As ever was of knight, or may
Be ever, seeing in war's bright way
　Praise knows not Balen's peer."

And Balen said, "Thou hast heard my name
Right: it repenteth me, though shame
May tax me not with base men's blame,
That ever, hap what will, I came
　Within this country; yet, being come,
For shame I may not turn again
Now, that myself and nobler men
May scorn me: now is more than then,
　And faith bids fear be dumb.

"Be it life or death, my chance I take,
Be it life's to build or death's to break:
And fall what may, me lists not make
Moan for sad life's or death's sad sake."
　Then looked he on his armour, glad
And high of heart, and found it strong:
And all his soul became a song
And soared in prayer that soared not long,
　For all the hope it had.

Then saw he whence against him came
A steed whose trappings shone like flame,
And he that rode him showed the same
Fierce colour, bright as fire or fame,
　But dark the visors were as night
That hid from Balen Balan's face,
And his from Balan: God's own grace
Forsook them for a shadowy space
　Where darkness cast out light.

The two swords girt that Balen bare
Gave Balan for a breath's while there
Pause, wondering if indeed it were
Balen his brother, bound to dare
　The chance of that unhappy quest:
But seeing not as he thought to see
His shield, he deemed it was not he,
And so, as fate bade sorrow be,
　They laid their spears in rest.

So mighty was the course they ran
With spear to spear so great of span,
Each fell back stricken, man by man,
Horse by horse, borne down: so the ban
   That wrought by doom against them wrought:
But Balen by his falling steed
Was bruised the sorer, being indeed
Way-weary, like a rain-bruised reed,
   With travel ere he fought.

And Balen rose again from swoon
First, and went toward him: all too soon
He too then rose, and the evil boon
Of strength came back, and the evil tune
   Of battle unnatural made again
Mad music as for death's wide ear
Listening and hungering toward the near
Last sigh that life or death might hear
   At last from dying men.

Balan smote Balen first, and clove
His lifted shield that rose and strove
In vain against the stroke that drove
Down: as the web that morning wove
   Of glimmering pearl from spray to spray
Dies when the strong sun strikes it, so
Shrank the steel, tempered thrice to show
Strength, as the mad might of the blow
   Shore Balen's helm away.

Then turning as a turning wave
Against the land-wind, blind and brave
In hope that dreams despair may save,
With even the unhappy sword that gave
   The gifts of fame and fate in one
He smote his brother, and there had nigh
Felled him: and while they breathed, his eye
Glanced up, and saw beneath the sky
   Sights fairer than the sun.

The towers of all the castle there
Stood full of ladies, blithe and fair
As the earth beneath and the amorous air
About them and above them were:
   So toward the blind and fateful fight
Again those brethren went, and sore
Were all the strokes they smote and bore,
And breathed again, and fell once more

To battle in their sight.

With blood that either spilt and bled
Was all the ground they fought on red,
And each knight's hauberk hewn and shred
Left each unmailed and naked, shed
  From off them even as mantles cast:
And oft they breathed, and drew but breath
Brief as the word strong sorrow saith,
And poured and drank the draught of death,
  Till fate was full at last.

And Balan, younger born than he
Whom darkness bade him slay, and be
Slain, as in mist where none may see
If aught abide or fall or flee,
  Drew back a little and laid him down,
Dying: but Balen stood, and said,
As one between the quick and dead
Might stand and speak, "What good knight's head
  Hath won this mortal crown?

"What knight art thou? for never I
Who now beside thee dead shall die
Found yet the knight afar or nigh
That matched me." Then his brother's eye
  Flashed pride and love; he spake and smiled
And felt in death life's quickening flame,
And answered: "Balan is my name,
The good knight Balen's brother; fame
  Calls and miscalls him wild."

The cry from Balen's lips that sprang
Sprang sharper than his sword's stroke rang.
More keen than death's or memory's fang,
Through sense and soul the shuddering pang
  Shivered: and scarce he had cried, "Alas
That ever I should see this day,"
When sorrow swooned from him away
As blindly back he fell, and lay
  Where sleep lets anguish pass.

But Balan rose on hands and knees
And crawled by childlike dim degrees
Up toward his brother, as a breeze
Creeps wingless over sluggard seas
  When all the wind's heart fails it: so
Beneath their mother's eyes had he,

A babe that laughed with joy to be,
Made toward him standing by her knee
   For love's sake long ago.

Then, gathering strength up for a space,
From off his brother's dying face
With dying hands that wrought apace
While death and life would grant them grace
   He loosed his helm and knew not him,
So scored with blood it was, and hewn
Athwart with darkening wounds: but soon
Life strove and shuddered through the swoon
   Wherein its light lay dim.

And sorrow set these chained words free:
"O Balan, O my brother! me
Thou hast slain, and I, my brother, thee
And now far hence, on shore and sea,
   Shall all the wide world speak of us."
"Alas," said Balan, "that I might
Not know you, seeing two swords were dight
About you; now the unanswering sight
   Hath here found answer thus.

"Because you bore another shield
Than yours, that even ere youth could wield
Like arms with manhood's tried and steeled
Shone as my star of battle-field,
   I deemed it surely might not be
My brother." Then his brother spake
Fiercely: "Would God, for thy sole sake,
I had my life again, to take
   Revenge for only thee!

"For all this deadly work was wrought
Of one false knight's false word and thought,
Whose mortal craft and counsel caught
And snared my faith who doubted nought,
   And made me put my shield away.
Ah, might I live, I would destroy
That castle for its customs: joy
There makes of grief a deadly toy,
   And death makes night of day."

"Well done were that, if aught were done
Well ever here beneath the sun,"
Said Balan: "better work were none:
For hither since I came and won

A woful honour born of death,
When here my hap it was to slay
A knight who kept this island way,
I might not pass by night or day
   Hence, as this token saith.

"No more shouldst thou, for all the might
Of heart and hand that seals thee knight
Most noble of all that see the light,
Brother, hadst thou but slain in fight
   Me, and arisen unscathed and whole,
As would to God thou hadst risen! though here
Light is as darkness, hope as fear,
And love as hate: and none draws near
   Save toward a mortal goal."

Then, fair as any poison-flower
Whose blossom blights the withering bower
Whereon its blasting breath has power,
Forth fared the lady of the tower
   With many a lady and many a knight,
And came across the water-way
Even where on death's dim border lay
Those brethren sent of her to slay
   And die in kindless fight.

And all those hard light hearts were swayed
With pity passing like a shade
That stays not, and may be not stayed,
To hear the mutual moan they made,
   Each to behold his brother die,
Saying, "Both we came out of one tomb,
One star-crossed mother's woful womb,
And so within one grave-pit's gloom
   Untimely shall we lie."

And Balan prayed, as God should bless
That lady for her gentleness,
That where the battle's mortal stress
Had made for them perforce to press
   The bed whence never man may rise
They twain, free now from hopes and fears,
Might sleep; and she, as one that hears,
Bowed her bright head: and very tears
   Fell from her cold fierce eyes.

Then Balen prayed her send a priest
To housel them, that ere they ceased

The hansel of the heavenly feast
That fills with light from the answering east
    The sunset of the life of man
Might bless them, and their lips be kissed
With death's requickening eucharist,
And death's and life's dim sunlit mist
    Pass as a stream that ran.

And so their dying rites were done:
And Balen, seeing the death-struck sun
Sink, spake as he whose goal is won:
"Now, when our trophied tomb is one,
    And over us our tale is writ,
How two that loved each other, two
Born and begotten brethren, slew
Each other, none that reads anew
    Shall choose but weep for it.

"And no good knight and no good man
Whose eye shall ever come to scan
The record of the imperious ban
That made our life so sad a span
    Shall read or hear, who shall not pray
For us for ever." Then anon
Died Balan; but the sun was gone,
And deep the stars of midnight shone,
    Ere Balen passed away.

And there low lying, as hour on hour
Fled, all his life in all its flower
Came back as in a sunlit shower
Of dreams, when sweet-souled sleep has power
    On life less sweet and glad to be.
He drank the draught of life's first wine
Again: he saw the moorland shine,
The rioting rapids of the Tyne,
    The woods, the cliffs, the sea.

The joy that lives at heart and home,
The joy to rest, the joy to roam,
The joy of crags and scaurs he clomb,
The rapture of the encountering foam
    Embraced and breasted of the boy,
The first good steed his knees bestrode,
The first wild sound of songs that flowed
Through ears that thrilled and heart that glowed,
    Fulfilled his death with joy.

So, dying not as a coward that dies
And dares not look in death's dim eyes
Straight as the stars on seas and skies
Whence moon and sun recoil and rise,
  He looked on life and death, and slept.
And there with morning Merlin came,
And on the tomb that told their fame
He wrote by Balan's Balen's name,
  And gazed thereon, and wept.

For all his heart within him yearned
With pity like as fire that burned.
The fate his fateful eye discerned
Far off now dimmed it, ere he turned
  His face toward Camelot, to tell
Arthur of all the storms that woke
Round Balen, and the dolorous stroke,
And how that last blind battle broke
  The consummated spell.

"Alas," King Arthur said, "this day
I have heard the worst that woe might say:
For in this world that wanes away
I know not two such knights as they."
  This is the tale that memory writes
Of men whose names like stars shall stand,
Balen and Balan, sure of hand,
Two brethren of Northumberland,
  In life and death good knights.

Algernon Charles Swinburne – A Short Biography

Algernon Charles Swinburne was born at 7 Chester Street, Grosvenor Place, in London, on April 5th, 1837. He was the eldest of six children born to Captain Charles Henry Swinburne and Lady Jane Henrietta, daughter of the 3rd Earl of Ashburnham, a wealthy Northumbrian family.

Swinburne spent his early years at East Dene in Bonchurch, on the Isle of Wight. As a child, Swinburne was nervous and frail, but also imbued with a nervous energy and fearlessness almost to the point of recklessness.

He was schooled at Eton College from 1849 to 1853. It was here that he first began to write poetry. He excelled at languages and whilst still at Eton won first prizes in both French and Italian.

From Eton he moved to Oxford where he attended at Balliol College from 1856. Here he met friends to whom he became closely attached, among them Dante Gabriel Rossetti, William Morris and Edward Burne-Jones, who in 1857, were painting their Arthurian murals on the walls of the Oxford Union. At

Oxford Swinburne was mentored by Benjamin Jowett, the master of Balliol College, who recognised his poetic talent and, intervening on his behalf, tried to keep him from being expelled when he celebrated the Italian patriot Orsini, and his failed attempt on the life of Napoleon III in 1858. Swinburne had to leave the Universcity for a few months due to this but returned in May, 1860 but never received a degree.

Summers were usually spent at Capheaton Hall in Northumberland, the house of his grandfather, Sir John Swinburne, 6th Baronet, who had a famous library and was himself President of the Literary and Philosophical Society in Newcastle upon Tyne.

Swinburne proudly considered himself a native of Northumberland and this is reflected in poems such as the intensely patriotic 'Northumberland' and 'Grace Darling'. He enjoyed riding across the moors and was, it was said, a daring horseman, as he moved 'through honeyed leagues of the northland border', as he remembered the Scottish border in his Recollections.

In the period from 1857 to 1860, Swinburne was one of a number of Pre-Raphaelite's who visited and became part of Lady Pauline Trevelyan's intellectual circle at Wallington Hall, a few miles west of Morpeth in Northumberland.

After leaving college, he moved to London and began his career in earnest as well as becoming a constant visitor to the Rossetti's house. To Rossetti Swinburne was his 'little Northumbrian friend', an affectionate reference to Swinburne's small stature—a mere five foot four. Whatever Swinburne lacked in height he made up for in poetic talent. However, with the burden of such great talent came the unveiling of a dark side that was to cause him pain and would, at times, threaten his very existence with all manner of self-inflicted pains through drink, drugs and sado-machoism.

In 1860 Swinburne published two verse dramas; The Queen Mother and Rosamond but it would not be until 1865 that Swinburne would achieve literary success with Atalanta in Calydon.

In 1861, Swinburne visited Menton on the French Riviera to recover from the effects of yet another period of excess use of alcohol, staying at the Villa Laurenti. From Menton, Swinburne then travelled on to Italy, where he journeyed widely.

After Elizabeth Rossetti's death from suicide in 1862, he and Rossetti moved to Tudor House at 16 Cheyne Walk in Chelsea. The stories that survive from his year with Rossetti are typical Swinburne. In one, Rossetti once had to tell him to keep down the noise — he and a boyfriend had been sliding naked down the bannisters and disturbing Rossetti's painting. He took a sardonic delight in what the critic and biographer, Cecil Lang, calls "Algernonic exaggeration": When people began to talk scathingly about his homosexuality and other sexual proclivities, he circulated a story that he had engaged in pederasty and bestiality with a monkey — and then eaten it. How many of the stories were true and how many invented is unclear. Oscar Wilde called him "a braggart in matters of vice, who had done everything he could to convince his fellow citizens of his homosexuality and bestiality without being in the slightest degree a homosexual or a bestialiser."

In December 1862, Swinburne accompanied Scott and his guests on a trip to Tynemouth. Scott writes in his memoirs that, as they walked by the sea, Swinburne declaimed the as yet unpublished 'Hymn to Proserpine' and 'Laus Veneris' in his lilting intonation, while the waves 'were running the whole length of the long level sands towards Cullercoats and sounding like far-off acclamations'.

Swinburne possessed a curious combination of frail health and strength. He was small and slightly built, but an excellent swimmer and the first to climb Culver Cliff on the Isle of Wight. He had an extremely excitable disposition: people who met him described him as a "demoniac boy" who would go skipping about the room declaiming poetry at the top of his voice. In this as in many things, moderation was not the standard for him. Excess was. Once or twice he had fits, thought to be epileptic, in public; but he made this condition much worse by drinking past excess to unconsciousness. More than once he was delivered to the door in the small of the night, dead drunk. Throughout the 1860s and '70s he rode an alcoholic cycle of dissolution, collapse, drying out at home in the country, then returning to London where he would begin the cycle all over again.

His mania for masochism, particularly flagellation, most probably started in early childhood at Eton and was encouraged by his later friendships with Richard Monckton Milnes (one of Tennyson's fellow Apostles), who introduced him to the works of the Marquis de Sade, and Richard Burton, the Victorian explorer and adventurer. Swinburne was an alcoholic and algolagniac (a desire for sexual gratification through inflicting pain on oneself or others; sadomasochism). He found life difficult, unfulfilling but still his poetic talents pushed to the fore.

Although Swinburne continued to publish some works in periodicals in 1865 he was granted recognition by both public and critics with Atalanta in Calydon written in the style of a classical Greek tragedy.

There followed "Laus Veneris" and Poems and Ballads (1866), with their sexually charged passages, absolutely decadent for polite Victorian society, which were attacked all the more violently as a result. The poems written in homage of Sappho of Lesbos such as "Anactoria" and "Sapphics" were especially savaged. The volume also contained poems such as "The Leper," "Laus Veneris," and "St Dorothy" which evoke both Swinburne's and a general Victorian fascination with the Middle Ages, and are explicitly mediaeval in style, tone and construction. With its publication came instant notoriety. He was now identified with indecent and decadent themes and the precept of art for art's sake.

Swinburne's meeting in 1867 with his long-time hero Mazzini, the Italian patriot living in England in exile, was the beginning of a poetical journey that now became more serious and more engaged with serious thought, initially leading to the political poems in the volume Songs Before Sunrise.

Also in 1867 he was introduced to Adah Isaacs Menken, the American actress, poet and circus rider, whose main fame seemed to be riding naked on a horse (in fact she wore tight nude coloured clothing) for her performance in the melodrama Mazeppa (itself based on a poem by Lord Byron). Although they had a short affair Adah's quote implies that Swinburne was not ready for a relationship that did not involve some self-sabotage; "I can't make him understand that biting's no use."

In 1879, with Swinburne nearly dead from alcoholism and dissolution, his legal advisor Theodore Watts-Dunton took him in, and was gradually successful in getting him to adapt to a healthier lifestyle. Swinburne lived the rest of his life at Watts-Dunton's house. He saw less and less of his old bohemian friends, who thought him a prisoner at The Pines, but his growing deafness also accounts for some of his decreased sociability. By now Swinburne was 42, and was moving from a young man of rebelliousness to a figure of social respectability. It was said of Watts-Dunton that he saved the man and killed the poet.

It is clear that Swinburne had an addictive personality, and clearly incapable of moderation in his pursuit of any chosen vices. This, of course, would both nourish and perhaps sabotage his poetic career. His poetry follows the somewhat clichéd pattern of early flourish and later decline; indeed some of the fresher pieces in the second and third series of Poems and Ballads (published in 1878 and 1889) were actually written during his days at Oxford. Nevertheless, his last collection, A Channel Passage, has some beautiful poems, including "The Lake of Gaube."

He is best remembered as the supreme technician in metre, with a versatility which exceeds even Tennyson's, but which lacks a corresponding emotional range. His obsessions are not widely enough shared; and if he cannot shock us by the strangeness of his desires nor the shrillness of his anti-theistical exclamations, often what remains is not enough to fully engage with the audience.

Swinburne is considered a poet of the decadent school, although he perhaps professed to more vice than he actually indulged in to advertise his deviance. Common gossip of the time reported that he also had a deep crush on the explorer Sir Richard Francis Burton, despite the fact that Swinburne himself abhorred travel. Fact and fiction are easily absorbed by the other so are difficult to untangle even now.

Many critics consider his mastery of vocabulary, rhyme and metre impressive, although he has also been criticised for his florid style and word choices that only fit the rhyme scheme rather than contributing to the meaning of the piece. A. E. Housman, although a critic, had great praise for his rhyming ability: to Swinburne the sonnet was child's play: the task of providing four rhymes was not hard enough, and he wrote long poems in which each stanza required eight or ten rhymes, and wrote them so that he never seemed to be saying anything for the rhyme's sake.

Throughout his career Swinburne published literary criticism of great worth. His deep knowledge of world literatures contributed to a critical style rich in quotation, allusion, and comparison. He is particularly noted for discerning studies of Elizabethan dramatists and of many English and French poets and novelists. As well he was a noted essayist and wrote two novels.

Swinburne was nominated for the Nobel Prize in Literature every year from 1903 to 1907 and then again in 1909.

H.P. Lovecraft, the master of the dark side and a decent poet himself, considered Swinburne "the only real poet in either England or America after the death of Mr. Edgar Allan Poe."

Swinburne was also responsible for devising a poetic form called the roundel, a variation of the French Rondeau form. In 1883 he published A Century of Roundels with several of the roundels dedicated to Dante's sister, the poet Christina Georgina Rossetti. Swinburne wrote to Edward Burne-Jones in 1883: "I have got a tiny new book of songs or songlets, in one form and all manner of metres ... just coming out, of which Miss Rossetti has accepted the dedication. I hope you and Georgie [his wife Georgiana] will find something to like among a hundred poems of nine lines each, twenty-four of which are about babies or small children".

Opinions of the Roundel poems move between those who find them captivating and brilliant, to others who find them merely clever and contrived. One of them, A Baby's Death, was set to music by the English composer Sir Edward Elgar as the song "Roundel: The little eyes that never knew Light".

After the first Poems and Ballads, Swinburne's later poetry was devoted more to philosophy and politics, including the unification of Italy, particularly in the volume Songs before Sunrise. He did not stop writing love poetry entirely, indeed it was only in 1882 that his great epic-length poem, Tristram of Lyonesse, was published, its contents lyrical rather than shocking. His versification, and especially his rhyming technique, remain of high quality to the end.

Algernon Charles Swinburne died of influenza, at the Pines in London on April 10th, 1909 at the age of 72. He was buried at St. Boniface Church, Bonchurch on the Isle of Wight.

Algernon Charles Swinburne – A Concise Bibliography

Verse Drama
The Queen Mother (1860)
Rosamond (1860)
Chastelard (1865)
Bothwell (1874)
Mary Stuart (1881)
Marino Faliero (1885)
Locrine (1887)
The Sisters (1892)
Rosamund, Queen of the Lombards (1899)

Poetry
Atalanta in Calydon (1865)*
Poems and Ballads (1866)
Songs Before Sunrise (1871)
Songs of Two Nations (1875)
Erechtheus (1876)*
Poems and Ballads, Second Series (1878)
Songs of the Springtides (1880)
Studies in Song (1880)
The Heptalogia, or the Seven against Sense. A Cap with Seven Bells (1880)
Tristram of Lyonesse (1882)
A Dark Month & Other Poems
A Century of Roundels (1883)
A Midsummer Holiday and Other Poems (1884)
Poems and Ballads, Third Series (1889)
Astrophel and Other Poems (1894)
The Tale of Balen (1896)
A Channel Passage and Other Poems (1904)

*Although formally tragedies, Atlanta in Calydon and Erechtheus are traditionally included with his poetry.

Criticism
William Blake: A Critical Essay (1868, new edition 1906)
Under the Microscope (1872)
George Chapman: A Critical Essay (1875)
Essays and Studies (1875)

A Note on Charlotte Brontë (1877)
A Study of Shakespeare (1880)
A Study of Victor Hugo (1886)
A Study of Ben Johnson (1889)
Studies in Prose and Poetry (1894)
The Age of Shakespeare (1908)
Shakespeare (1909)

Major Collections

The Poems of Algernon Charles Swinburne, 6 vols. 1904.
The Tragedies of Algernon Charles Swinburne, 5 vols. 1905.
The Complete Works of Algernon Charles Swinburne, 20 vols. Bonchurch Edition. 1925-7.
The Swinburne Letters, 6 vols. 1959-62.

www.ingramcontent.com/pod-product-compliance
Lightning Source LLC
Chambersburg PA
CBHW060053050426
42448CB00011B/2430